Wildlife in Central America 1;

25 Amazing Animals Living in Tropical Rainforest and River Habitats

Text and Photography by Cyril Brass

Thank you for purchasing this book and in doing so

Receive a FREE ebook copy of the classic wildlife adventure:

"The Jungle Book"

Go to

www.wildlifearoundtheworld.com

Please visit our website at www.wildlifearoundtheworld.com for more detailed wildlife information and stunning photo image books.

Front cover image: Green Basilisk
Back cover images: Three-Toed Sloth and Red-Eyed Tree Frog

Wildlife Around the World Series

Wildlife in Central America 1;

25 Amazing Animals Living in Tropical Rainforest and River Habitats

Text and Photography by Cyril Brass

Table of Contents

Introduction

Welcome to Wildlife in Central America 1; 25 Amazing Animals living in Tropical Rainforest and River Habitats part of the Wildlife around the World Series.

This book is a great introduction to the wildlife living in Central America. With easy-to-read text and eye-catching images, curious readers will identify and learn about 25 wildlife species living in the rainforests and rivers of Central America.

The number of wildlife species living in Central America is so extensive that we cannot provide images and information on all of them in this book. Included within this book is a representation of the thousands and thousands of amazing animals that live in and around the tropical rainforests and rivers of Central America.

Stunning colorful photos and descriptive text fills every engaging page providing an exciting look at the wide variety of fascinating and unusual creatures; from colorful scarlet macaws living high in the treetops to tiny strawberry poison dart frogs living on the forest ground; from non-aggressive spectacled caimans living in the rivers and streams to venomous eyelash palm pit vipers resting on branches of trees in the dense rainforest.

These fun-filled pages provide facts and images about each of the 25 animals included in this book; what they look like, what habitat they live in, what they eat, how the parents take care of their young, how they defend themselves in the wild, and many more interesting details.

More and more readers will understand and appreciate the precious world around us by exploring and learning about the many amazing wild creatures living in different regions of the world. This book will appeal to wildlife enthusiasts and animal lovers of all ages.

About Central America

Central America is the southern geographical region in the continent of North America.

Seven countries that make up Central America: Belize, Guatemala, El Salvador, Honduras, Nicaragua, Costa Rica and Panama.

The size of Central America is 523,780 square kilometers (202,230 square miles) which is 0.1% of the Earth's surface.

The Central America land formation connects Mexico in North America to Columbia in South America.

There are bodies of water on both sides of Central America; the Pacific Ocean is on the west side and the Caribbean Sea is on the east side.

Central America is one of the most bio-diverse regions on the planet providing a wide variety of natural habitats and ecosystems. The area provides homes and food for an abundant number of wildlife species in this small geographical region.

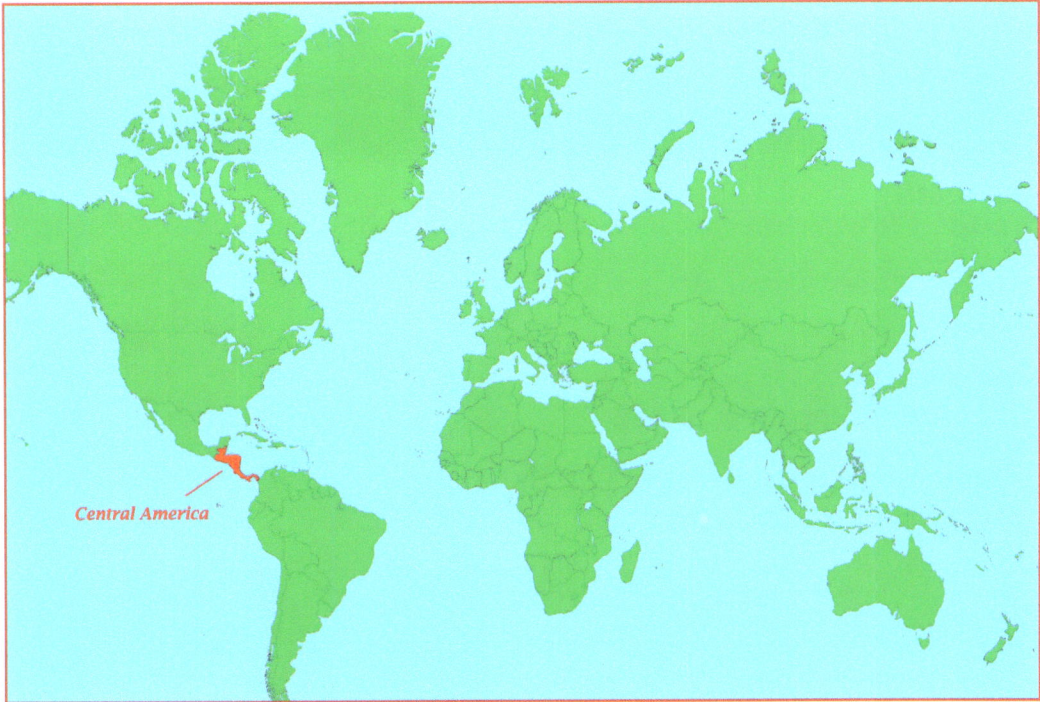

Central America

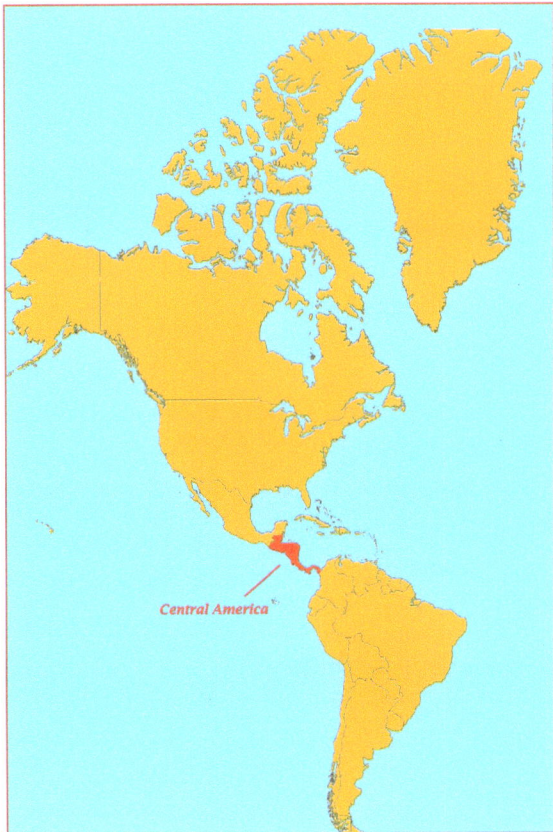

Central America

White-Faced Capuchin Monkey

(Cebus Capucinus)

The White-Faced Capuchin Monkey is a highly intelligent mammal able to use objects like sticks and rocks for specific purposes.

These diurnal creatures spend each day traveling through the trees and vegetation searching for food. They check all levels of the forest from ground level to the forest canopy. They are omnivores, who eat a variety of fruits, flowers, seeds, insects and invertebrates.

They are social animals often seen playing in the trees, running on the ground or quietly grooming each other.

The White-Faced Capuchin Monkey has a long prehensile tail that is used to grip tightly onto tree branches for support while reaching for food or swinging from branch to branch.

Females give birth to a single offspring every two years. The newborn baby clings to the mother's chest until it grows bigger when it moves on to the mother's back.

The youngster will hang out with the mother until it is able to live on its own. During this time, it learns and develops necessary eating, moving and survival skills.

This species of primate has a vital role in the rainforest. They disperse pollen and seeds of plants while moving throughout the jungle habitat.

Three-Toed Sloth

(Bradypus Variegatus)

The Three-Toed Sloth, like all sloth species, is the slowest mammal on earth. It is so slow that algae grow on its furry coats giving it a greenish appearance.

This sloth species is named by the number of fingers and toes they have; three fingers and three toes. The close relative, the Two-Toed Sloth has two fingers and three toes.

The long, hooked claws on each finger and toe are well suited for an arboreal life.

Nearly all of its life is spent hanging upside down from branches high in the tree tops. It eats, sleeps and reproduces while hanging upside down.

To conserve energy in the body, it sleeps fifteen to twenty hours every day.

The Three-Toed Sloth is an excellent climber and swimmer, but on land, its body structure does not allow it to walk on its arms and legs.

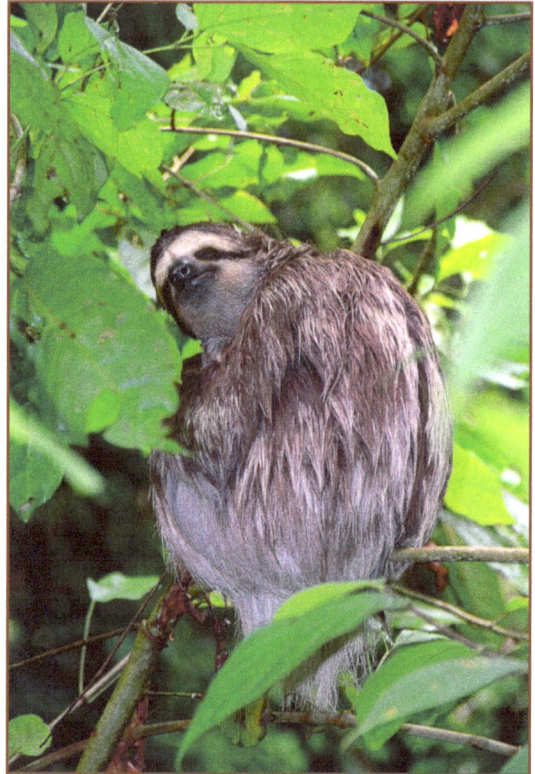

This tree dweller only climbs down to the forest floor once a week to quickly go to the bathroom. This is a time when it is in the most danger, extremely vulnerable to predator attacks.

MAMMALS

Central American Agouti

(Dasyprocta Punctata)

The Central American Agouti is a small mammal that live on the forest floor.

These rodents look similar to their close relative of the guinea pig having short legs and a tail. They have slender bodies covered by glossy fur that is two colors (red and brown).

These herbivores eat fruit, nuts, seeds, leaves and roots. They sit on their hind legs while eating food which they hold with their front feet.

They are equipped with sharp incisor teeth that enable them to crack the shell of hard nuts.

Sometimes, Agoutis act like forest gardeners. They store nuts and seeds in the ground for meals to eat later, but if they forget about the stored food, the nuts and seeds grow into new plants.

When these terrestrial animals sense danger, they freeze, not moving any part of their body, hoping their predators will not see them amongst the fallen leaves and branches.

White-Nose Coatimundi
(Nasua Narica)

The White-Nose Coatimundi spends most of the day foraging on the forest floor for food, digging through fallen leaves.

These omnivores will eat lizards, birds, and fruit and use their long mobile snouts to dig for insects and roots.

This mammal has a long nose, an elongated body, and a long bushy tail banded with dark rings. Its thick fur coat has a range of colors from yellowish brown or reddish brown to black.

When a White-Nose Coatimundi walks, its long ringed tail is held vertical waving slowly above the ground cover.

They travel in large groups called "bands" of up to twenty or more females with their young. The males are solitary creatures and join the bands only during the mating season.

These raccoon relatives are agile climbers. If threatened by predators, they can quickly escape into nearby trees.

They spend the evenings sleeping on branches high in the tree canopy.

Neotropical River Otter

(Lontra Longicaudis)

The Neotropical River Otter lives at the edge of lagoons, swamps, rivers, and streams within dense forest and vegetation habitats.

Its long streamlined body is covered in short dark brown fur. It possesses a soft fur undercoat that is covered with guard hairs that helps to keep the undercoat dry when the animal goes into the water.

This otter does not have an insulating layer of fat, so it depends on its fur to keep warm and dry.

This semi-aquatic mammal possesses powerful webbed claws on its feet and a long strong tail that acts like a propeller allowing it to be an efficient and fast swimmer.

Unlike other otter species, the Neotropical River Otters are solitary animals. They are shy creatures and stay away from places where lots of people are located.

Neotropical River Otters are extremely rare in the wild as this otter species is highly endangered.

Red-Eyed Tree Frog

(Agalychnis Callidryas)

The big bright red eyes of the Red-Eyed Tree Frog are believed to be used for protecting themselves from approaching predators. This sudden flash of bright red in the trees startles the birds or snakes. The attackers pause for a second and the frog is then able to quickly leap to safety.

When this tree frog moves through its arboreal habitat, its colorful bodies are visible with bright blue and yellow patterns on their sides. Its large webbed feet are a bright orange.

Despite its bright coloration on the body, legs and eyes, the Red-Eyed Tree Frog is non-venomous, unlike other colorful tropical frogs which are highly poisonous.

During the day it sleeps stuck to the underside of leaves. Its eyes are closed and all the body colors are hidden, making it well camouflaged with the surrounding vegetation.

This nocturnal amphibian searches for food in the dark. It clings to forest branches waiting to strike out with its long sticky tongue to catch crickets and moths.

Strawberry Poison Dart Frog

(Oophaga Pumilio, Dendrobates Pumilio)

The Strawberry Poison Dart Frog's head and body are bright red, marked with small dark random spots. The forearms and hind limbs are colored in bright blue or purplish blue.

These blue legs give them the common name of the "Blue-Jeans" frogs.

This bright coloration is used to scare away potential predators. It is a warning sign to other animals that they are poisonous so do not come close. Their skin excretes toxins which can be harmful and even deadly to some attackers.

This poison dart frog species lives on the ground and in the lower vegetation of the rainforest.

The females lay the eggs on leaves on the forest floor. Once the eggs hatch, the parents carry the hatchlings on their backs to pools of water higher in the vegetation.

These tiny (2.5 centimeters (1.0 inch)) and vocal amphibians are territorial animals protecting an area of one square meter in size. They are usually heard before they are seen.

Smokey Jungle Frog

(Leptodactylus Pentadactylus)

The Smokey Jungle Frog is one of the biggest frogs in the world with a body length up to 20.0 centimeters (7.9 inches).

This nocturnal frog is mostly seen after dark when it is searching for food. It spends its days in burrows, under logs, or hidden in leaf litter.

The Smokey Jungle Frog waits to ambush its prey. It is a voracious eater, consuming almost anything it can catch.

This carnivore will eat other frog species, snakes, lizards, small birds as well as big invertebrates.

This terrestrial amphibian defends itself by releasing irritating toxins from its skin causing the predator to quickly drop it. It also inflates its lungs which elevates its body on all four limbs giving it a much larger appearance to potential attackers.

In shallow water, females lay approximately 1,000 eggs in floating foam nests, which are created by the male.

AMPHIBIANS

Spectacled Caiman

(Caiman Crocodilus)

The Spectacled Caiman is related to the American Crocodile but is much smaller in size reaching up to about 2.7 meters (8.6 feet). The American Crocodiles can reach up to 7.0 meters (21.0 feet).

The name is derived from the bony ridges around the front of the eyes, appearing like a pair of spectacles.

These non-aggressive reptiles prefer freshwater habitats. They rarely leave the water. During the day they lie quietly in water with only their eyes and nostrils exposed above the surface. At night they hunt for food.

Spectacled Caiman are responsible parents, who closely guard the nest of eggs which are located in a large mound of soil and plant material built close to rivers and streams.

When the babies are born, the hatchlings call out to their parents who dig open the nest. Using their mouths, the parents carry their offspring to the nearby water.

Green Basilisk

(Basiliscus Plumifrons)

The adult male Green Basilisk possesses a distinctive sail-like crest on its head, and along the back and tail. The female's crest is much smaller in size.

The brilliant green coloration with blue and white spots on its sides and tail provides excellent camouflage allowing it to easily blend into the vegetation.

Using its specially designed long-toed, wide feet and a unique running style, these reptiles have the ability to run on the surface of water for a considerable distance.

These semi-arboreal lizards rest on logs, rocks and vegetation close to rivers, streams and ponds. This position allows for a quick escape from predators. They can scurry into the dense bushes, dive into the water or run on top of the water.

Green Basilisks are omnivores that feed on a variety of plant material, insects and arthropods, but will also eat small lizards and fish.

Green Iguana

(Iguana Iguana)

The Green Iguana has a dinosaur-like appearance possessing a tall crest consisting of long comb-like scales from its neck to its tail.

They have a large dewlap that hangs under the chin from the throat. Below the ear on each side of the head is a large, distinctive circular scale.

This cold-blooded reptile spends most of its time stretching out on branches, high in the trees, basking in the hot sun. It positions itself on vegetation at the edge of the rainforest close to water.

The Green Iguana is primarily an herbivore, but it will eat insects and worms.

Once the eggs are laid by the females, there is no more parental care by either the mother or father.

Male Iguanas can be seen bobbing their heads in territorial displays to scare off potential attackers or to attract females for mating. The male's body turns from green to orange during the mating season.

Eyelash Palm Pit Viper

(Bothriechis Schlegelii)

The Eyelash Palm Pit Viper is a small and extremely venomous snake. It grows to a length up to 80.0 centimeters (31.5 inches) which is short compared to other snake species. The name is derived from the two to three pointed hood-like scales projecting over each eye appearing as "eyelashes".

They have two heat-sensitive pits between the eyes and nostrils. The scales of this snake are rough and sharp to touch, unlike most other snakes whose scales are smooth.

This species of pit viper comes in a variety of colors from yellow, green, and rust, to brown, gray and light blue. Despite all those colors they are still well camouflaged animals, making them difficult to spot among the dense low lying branches, vines and vegetation of the rainforests.

This non aggressive arboreal creature spends most of its life resting motionless on tree branches, tree trunks, tropical flowers and fruit awaiting their prey. Eyelash Palm Pit Vipers are carnivores preying on small mammals, birds, lizards and frogs. They attack their prey quickly, inject a hemotoxic venom with their very long fangs, wait for it to die and then swallow it.

The females incubate the eggs internally for six months. The eggs hatch inside the female where they complete their development. There are two to twenty live young per brood, all looking identical to their parents.

Green Vine Snake

(Oxybelis Fulgidus)

The Green Vine Snake is an arboreal snake with a thin green body that looks like a growing vine and its pointed head resembles a leaf. This leafy coloration allows this snake to be well camouflaged in dense vegetation.

Its long, slender body may reach up to 2.0 meters (6.5 feet).

The upper part of the body is bright green and the underside is yellowish-green. A narrow, yellowish-white stripe runs along each side of the body and tail.

This non-venomous reptile has an aero-dynamic shaped head, a prominent pointed nose, a large mouth that extends the length of the head, and two large fangs at the back of the mouth.

The tail is prehensile allowing this tree snake to hold on to branches or vines while reaching for prey.

The Green Vine Snake is an ambush predator using a sit and wait approach to hunt for its food. This carnivore eat frogs, lizards and small birds.

Scarlet Macaw

(Ara Macao)

The Scarlet Macaw is a beautifully colored member of the parrot family. This large bird has bright red plumage covering its head and body with big patches of yellow and blue on its wings and tail.

The big, powerful beak is able to easily crack open nuts and seeds. The massive hooked beak is white on the top and black on bottom. It is very efficient for breaking open nuts and fruit.

These birds eat a diverse range of wild nuts, fruits and flowers. Unlike some macaws, this macaw species is not dependent on one food source so they will travel long distances from their nesting sites to different feeding locations.

They have gripping toes that are able to grasp branches tightly and hold onto smaller items so they can examine them more closely.

Scarlet Macaws are intelligent social birds who are seen in small groups during the day. They form larger flocks when roosting high in the trees for the night.

Their loud calls and squawks can be heard echoing through the forest.

These are monogamous creatures having a single lifetime partner. Together, they raise their young in huge hollow trees.

BIRDS

Keel-Billed Toucan

(Ramphastos Sulfuratus)

The Keel-Billed Toucan or Rainbow-Billed Toucan is known for its long beak that is colored in fascinating shades of blues, greens, yellows, oranges and red on the tip.

Although the bill appears thick and awkward, it is actually slender and lightweight consisting of a strong honeycomb patterned bone structure inside.

They use their beaks as a tool to reach fruits on branches that are too small to support their weight. With the tip of the beak, they pick the juicy fruits and seeds, then flick the fruit or seeds into the air and catch the food in their open mouths.

These tropical birds have a unique flight pattern of wingbeat bursts alternating with long descending glides.

Keel-Billed Toucans build their nests in vacant tree holes, where both parents take care of the two to four eggs and hatchlings.

Anhinga
(Anhinga Anhinga)

The Anhinga is a very distinctive looking water bird that has a snake-like head and neck. Its appearance and posture is similar to the neo-tropical Cormorant.

The modified vertebrate in the neck allows it to bend back in an S-shaped position. This physical adaptation allows the bird to quickly thrust its bill forward spearing its prey.

Unlike other wetland birds, the unique plumage of the Anhinga allows the feathers to become waterlogged quickly, helping them to be in a low position when swimming with only the head and neck exposed above the surface of the water.

This position gives the appearance of a snake moving in the water and has given the Anhinga another name of "Snake Bird".

The Anhinga must dry their feathers before they are able to fly. They perch themselves on a log or branch in an upright posture with wings spread out absorbing the heat from the tropical sun.

These feathered creatures do not hunt like most other wetland birds that search for prey from above the water surface. Instead, Anhinga dive underwater to hunt for small fish and spear them with their sharply pointed bills.

Northern Jacana

(Jacana Spinosa)

The Northern Jacana is a small wading bird common in shallow wetland habitats. It grows in size up to 23.0 centimeters (9.0 Inches).

It has a distinctive chestnut brown body and wings, a black head and neck with a yellow frontal shield and bill.

These water birds have extremely long toes and toenails which allow them to walk on lily pads, water hyacinths and other floating vegetation.

While walking on the floating vegetation, they search for aquatic insects, invertebrates, tiny fish and snails.

The females are territorial birds defending an area that contains one to four males. The females mate with all the males in her territory.

It is the males who take care of the eggs and hatchlings. The female's only parental responsibility is to guard the nests from predators while the males incubate the eggs. The male raises the young after they hatch.

Green Heron

(Butorides Virescens)

The Green Heron is a small water bird with a grayish dark green back, maroon or reddish brown neck, black on the top of its head and yellow legs.

As it waits patiently for prey to approach, it crouches with its body low and with its head close to its body.

These solitary birds are found in aquatic habitats with shallow water providing opportunities for catching small fish, shrimp, insects and frogs.

Even though these herons live near marshes, rivers and ponds, they do not wade in the water for long periods of time like other larger heron species. Instead, they prefer to stand on vegetation, tree branches or on the ground close to the water's edge.

When hunting for food, Green Herons sometime use tools as bait and lures including insects, feathers and twigs to catch meals.

A Green Heron lays two to four eggs in a nest built in the vegetation near water.

Owl Butterfly

(Caligo Eurilochus)

The Owl Butterfly is one of the largest butterflies in the world with a wingspan of 13.7 - 18.3 centimeters (5.4 – 7.2 inches).

This species is identified by the blue-purple color of the upper forewing and cream band on the upper hindwing.

The most distinguishing feature is the two large yellow-ringed eyespots on the underside of the wings. These spots represent owl eyes which may scare off potential predators. They also provide a target that attracts predators away from the butterfly's body.

The Owl Butterfly flutters through the forest understory with slow flaps of its large wings. Upon landing, it rests on tree trunks and branches with its wings closed blending in with the surrounding colors.

The large caterpillars are gregarious eaters, consuming leaves from their host plants such as heliconius, bananas and cyclanths. Adults, using their proboscis, feed on rotting fruit, tree sap, mammal dung and carrion as there are few flowers in the rainforests.

The Owl Butterflies are diurnal insects, active during the day from dawn to dusk.

Blue Morpho Butterfly

(Morpho Peleides)

The iridescent blue wings of the Blue Morpho Butterfly create brilliant flashes of blue against the lush green vegetation of the rainforest. This metallic shiny blue covers the upper wing surface.

The underside of the wings appear like the surrounding foliage of browns, grays, blacks and reds. The underside is marked with several eyespots.

These giant butterflies are forest dwellers but will travel into sunny open areas to warm their bodies by the sun. Males are territorial creatures defending their home region from rival males.

They have a fast irregular floppy flight pattern as they travel along the rainforest trails and open waterways. The large forewings can reach lengths of 7.5 centimeters (3.0 inches)

An adult uses its proboscis to feed on rotting fruit, tree sap and carrion. It does not visit flowers for the sweet juicy nectar. The adult drinks its food and the caterpillar eats its food.

Blue Morpho Butterflies do not possess toxins like other tropical butterflies. They rely on their erratic flight pattern as an effective defense against predatory birds, making them difficult to chase and catch.

Giant Red-Winged Grasshopper

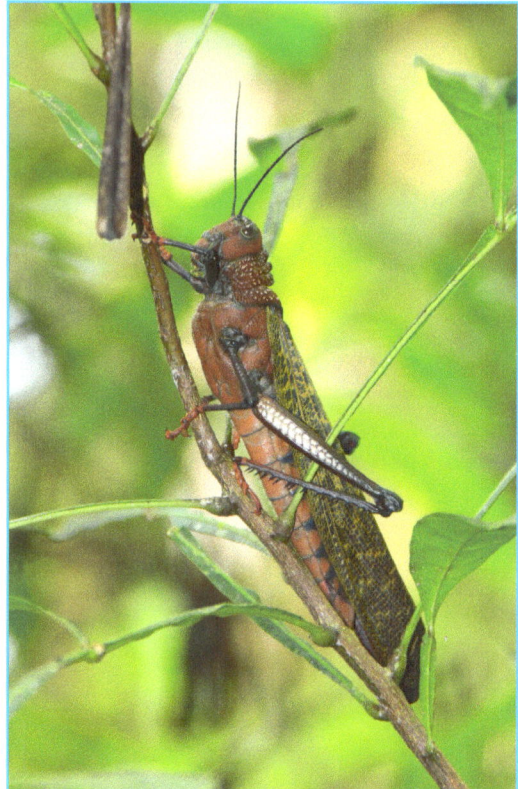

(Tropidacris Cristata)

The Giant Red-Winged Grasshopper is one of the largest grasshoppers in the world. These impressive insects can reach lengths of 16.0 centimeters (6.3 inches).

Unlike the adults, the young nymphs are yellow and black. As they go through the maturing phase of life, these warning colors transform into dark brown blending into their habitats. They look like two completely different species.

The adults have two pairs of large red wings with a wingspan up to 24.0 centimeters (9.4 inches). The forewings resemble leaves.

These tropical grasshoppers are herbivores feeding on a variety of plants in the rainforest.

The males vibrate their wings making loud sounds to attract females for mating.

Giant Red-Winged Grasshoppers use their powerful hind legs, which are covered with sharp spines to kick predators that come too close. They will also defend themselves by spitting a brown bitter liquid at their attackers.

Rhinoceros Beetle

(Megasoma Occidentalis)

The Rhinoceros Beetle is named for its long, upward curving horn, which only the male possesses.

The large dome-shaped body, barb-like appendages and head supporting different sized horns makes these creatures extremely unique in the animal world. These big beetles reach sizes of 0.8-1.2 centimeters (2-3 inches).

The females' choice of mates is determined by who has the best resources which is the best feeding sites that consist of large decaying trees where offspring can be produced.

The larva stage of the Rhinoceros Beetle lasts up to four years before it emerges as a more threatening full grown horned beetle.

Despite their threatening appearance, the horns are used for battle with other males for control over food-rich territories and mating grounds. They are not used to fight off predators.

In proportion to their own size, the Rhinoceros Beetles are considered one of the strongest animals in the world, capable of lifting 850 times their body weight. If a human had this strength, they would be able to lift a 65 ton object.

INSECTS

Leaf-Cutter Ant
(Atta Cephalotes)

The Leaf-Cutter Ant is a hardworking insect getting its name by the way it cuts leaves, which it then carries back to the colony. It carves a circular-shaped, green chunk from a leaf and carries it upright in its jaws.

Endless lines of worker ants march their way down the tree trunk, hauling their cargo along well-groomed jungle paths free of debris and obstructions.

At the colony, the chunks of leaves are chewed by the ants but not eaten. Instead, compost is created on which they grow a nutritional fungus. It is the fungus that the ants eat and feed to their young. The underground colony is a fungus farm.

These non-stop workers can be easily found in the rainforest by the endless trail of leaf carriers; from the leafy tree branches to the worn trails on the ground to the mouth of the underground colony.

There are five different sizes of Leaf-Cutter Ants. Each has a specific job in the organized colony; Minims (Caretakers), Minors (Guard Patrollers), Mediaes (Foragers), Majors (Soldiers) and Queen.

Orange-Kneed Tarantula

(Megaphobema Mesomelas)

For having an intimidating appearance, the Orange-Kneed Tarantula is a fragile creature and steps delicately around the forest floor habitat.

A warning sign that a tarantula is becoming aggressive is when it rears up on its back legs, sometimes adding an angry hiss.

The spider's fangs are underneath its head so the spider needs to come down on top of its prey.

While the venom of a tarantula is not fatal, the bite can still be deep and painful. The venom is used to stun the prey and to defend themselves when attacked.

These terrestrial spiders are hunters, not spinners. They do not spin a silk web to catch their prey, as most arachnid species are commonly known for.

They dig a burrow in the ground or build nests made of leaves, lined with silk.

This arachnid uses its front legs as antennae to feel around in front of its body. This method gives the spider a stronger sense of its surroundings than is provided by its eight small eyes.

Orange-Kneed Tarantulas are nocturnal creatures, emerging at dusk or into the night to mate and hunt. The males are territorial animals defending their territory from other males.

ARACHNIDS

Large Forest-Floor Millipede

(Nyssodesmus Python)

Despite its name the Large Forest-Floor Millipede or Python Millipede does not have 1,000 legs, but between 80 and 400 legs depending on the specific species.

They are slow moving creatures incapable of crawling fast with so many legs to coordinate. These terrestrial invertebrates can reach sizes up to 10-12 centimeters (3.9-4.7 inches).

They possess flattened, cylindrical, long bodies composed of twenty or so narrow segments colored in tan with brown or black stripes. Each body segment has two pairs of legs except for the first three segments.

Unlike centipedes, millipedes cannot bite, pinch or sting to protect themselves. Their primary defense is to release from their body bad smelling poisonous liquid secretions containing hydrogen cyanide. A second defense from danger is for them to curl up in a tight spiral coil hiding their delicate legs and soft underbelly under the armored exterior shell.

These scavengers are both herbivores and detritvores consuming live plant material and decomposing materials like rotting leaves and decaying wood.

The Large Forest-Floor Millipedes provide an important role in the rainforests by helping break down dead and decaying plant matter returning essential nutrients back into the ecosystem.

Glossary of Terms

Amphibian (n)	an animal that is able to live both in water and on land
Arachnid (n)	group of small animals similar to insects but having four pairs of legs
Arboreal (adj)	the lifestyle of an animal living in trees
Arthropod (n)	an invertebrate animal that has an external skeleton, a segmented body and jointed limbs
Basking (v)	the behavior of resting in the sun as a way of raising the body temperature, commonly performed by cold-blooded animals
Burrow (n)	a hole or tunnel dug in the ground by a small animal
Camouflage (n)	the appearance of an animal when placed against a background which makes the animal difficult or impossible to see
Carnivore (n)	an animal that eats meat
Carrion (n)	the flesh of dead animals
Colony (n)	a group of the same kind of animals living together
Dewlap (n)	a fold of fleshy skin that hangs down from the chin and throat area
Diurnal (adj)	an animal that is active during daylight hours
Ecosystem (n)	a community of organisms and their physical environment interacting as a unit
Endangered (adj)	at high risk and threatened with extinction
Flock (n)	a group of birds
Forewing (n)	the two front wings of a four-winged insect
Gregarious (adj)	tending to live in groups
Habitat (n)	an ecological or environmental area where a particular species of animal lives
Herbivore (n)	an animal that eats plant materials
Insect (n)	an animal that has an exoskeleton, a three-part body, three pairs of jointed legs, compound eyes and one pair of antennae
Invertebrate (n)	an animal that lacks a spinal column
Iridescent (adj)	shining with many different colors when seen from different angles
Larva (n)	the immature stage of an animal prior to metamorphosis
Mammal (n)	an animal that gives live birth (not from eggs) and feeds them on milk from female's own body

Metamorphosis (n)	the process by which the creature like an insect or amphibian changes its form from an egg to a caterpillar to a cocoon to a moth or butterfly; from an egg to a nymph to an adult; or from an egg to a tadpole to a frog
Monogamous (adj)	a single female and male who create a lifelong bond with each other and do not have multiple mates
Nocturnal (adj)	an animal that is active at night
Nymph (n)	an immature form of an insect
Offspring (n)	the animals resulting from reproduction
Omnivore (n)	an animal that eats a variety of food that may include plant, animals, algae, fungi and bacteria
Plumage (n)	the feathers of a bird
Poisonous (adj)	containing poison
Predator (n)	an animal that hunts other animals for food
Prehensile tail (n)	a tail that can be curled to grip a branch and that can support part of all of the animal's weight
Prey (n)	an animal that is attacked by another animal
Proboscis (n)	a slender tubular organ on the head of an invertebrate used for sucking or piercing
Rainforest (n)	a forest located in a hot region of the world that receives a lot of rain
Reptile (n)	an animal whose blood temperature changes according to the outside temperature and whose body is covered by hard material such as scales or plates
Semi-Aquatic (adj)	able to live both on land and in the water
Solitary (adj)	living alone without others
Species (n)	a group of closely related animals that possess common characteristics and freely interbreed in nature and produce fertile offspring
Terrestrial (adj)	living on the ground
Territorial (adj)	the actions taken to defend a habitat or region against other animals of the same species
Toxin (n)	a substance produced by a living creature that is poisonous to other creatures
Tree canopy (n)	the upper layer or habitat zone formed by the tops of trees
Understory (n)	smaller trees, shrubs and vegetation that grow within a taller forest
Venomous (adj)	a creature the possesses a poisonous substance used for protection against predators
Vertebrate (n)	an animal that possesses a backbone or spinal column
Wetland (n)	land areas such as marshes and swamps where the water covers the soil or is near the surface of the soil all year
Wildlife (n)	non-domesticated animal species living in nature

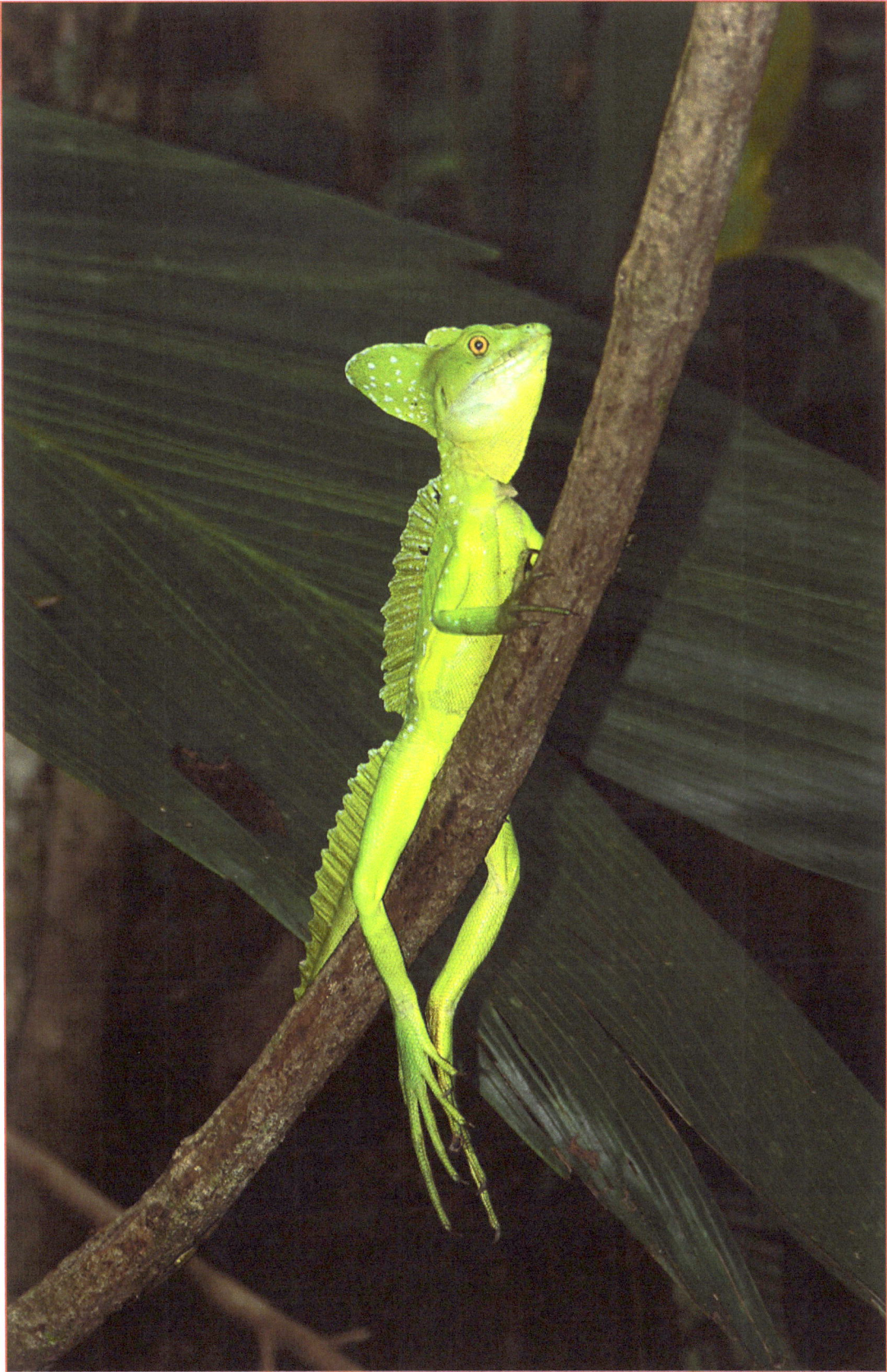

Index

A

Amphibian 20,22,24,58
Arachnid 54,58
Arboreal 12,20,28,32,34,58
Arthropod 28,58

B

Basking 30,58
Bird 16,20,24,32,34,36,38,
40,42,44,48,58
Burrow 24,54,58

C

Camouflage 20,28,32,34,58
Carnivore 24,32,34,58
Carrion 46,48,58
Colony 52,58

D

Detritvore 57,58
Dewlap 30,58
Diurnal 10,46,58

E

Ecosystem 8,56,58
Endangered 18,58

F

Forewing 46,58

G

Gregarious 46,58

H

Habitat 6,8,18,26,42,44,50,
54,58,61
Herbivore 14,30,50,56,58

I

Insect 10,16,28,30,42,44,46,
50,58
Invertebrate 24,42,56,58
Iridescent 48,58

L

Larva 50,58

M

Mammal 10,12,14,16,18,32,
46,58
Metamorphosis 58
Monogamous 36,59

N

Nocturnal 20,24,54,59
Nymph 50,59

O

Offspring 10,26,51,59

P

Plumage 36,40,59
Poisonous 20,22,56,59
Predator 12,14,16,20,22,24,
28,34,42,46,48,50,51,59
Prehensile tail 10,34,59
Prey 24,32,34,40,44,54,59
Proboscis 46,48,59

R

Rainforest 6,10,22,30,32,46,
50,52,56,59
Reptile 26,28,30,32,34,59

S

Semi-Aquatic 18,59
Solitary 16,18,44,59
Species 6,8,10,12,18,22,24,
32,36,44,46,50,54,56

T

Terrestrial 14,24,54,56,59
Territorial 22,30,42,48,54,
59
Tree canopy 16,59

U

Understory 46,59

V

Venomous 6,20,32,34,54,59
Vertebrate 40, 59

W

Wetland 40,42,59
Wildlife 6, 8, 59

About the Photographer and Author

Published author and freelance wildlife photographer Cyril Brass presents a combination of informative text and unique photographs detailing many interesting characteristics and behaviors about many wildlife species living in the Tropical Rainforest and River Habitats of Central America.

Cyril has always been interested in wild animals in far-off countries. Once he caught the travel bug he was able to learn and photograph first-hand, encountering many wildlife species he had only read about or seen on TV.

For many years, Cyril has been exploring wildlife all around the world; from sloths and toucans in the tropical rainforests of Central America to elephants and lions on the savannas of East Africa.

His wildlife book series covers informative details and colorful images of many amazing animals living in different habitats and regions around the world for readers of all ages to enjoy.

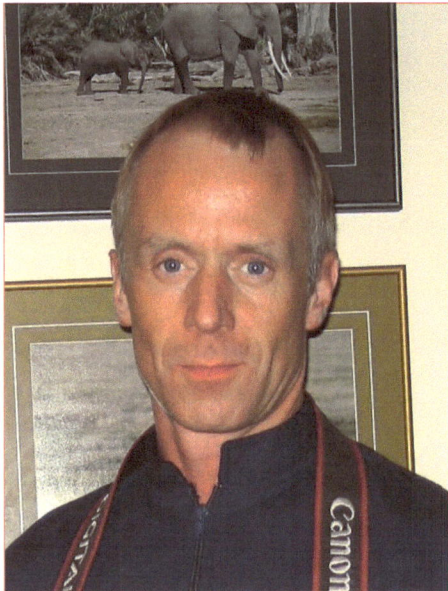